ALL
WALLY

A DRABBLE BOOK
BY KEVIN FAGAN

ISBN: 978-1976050923
ISBN-13: 1976050928

ABOUT WALLY

Wally is the hyper-hilarious wiener dog from the DRABBLE comic strip.

Whether protecting the Drabble home from badgers, the Easter bunny, or empty water bottles, Wally can always be counted on to give it his all. He is loyal, intelligent, fearless, and funny! Wally makes a great comfort pet for Ralph (or maybe it's vice-versa).

KEVIN FAGAN

All Wally: A DRABBLE Book

KEVIN FAGAN

Other DRABBLE books by Kevin Fagan

The First Book of Drabble
Basic Drabble
Drabble: In The Fast Lane
Dad, I'm an Elvis Impersonator
Son of Drabble
Drabble: Mall Cops, Ducks, and Fenderheads
Drabblations
Drabble: Who Wants to be a Fenderhead
A Drabble Family Christmas Tale
Wally's Wienerful World of Golf

KEVIN FAGAN

DRABBLE By FAGAN ®

Wally's DOG TRAINING GUIDE

HOW TO TEACH YOUR DOG TO SIT

WHEN YOUR DOG IS STANDING, SAY "SIT!"

TAKE A DOG TREAT AND HOLD IT NEAR HIS NOSE SO HE CAN SEE IT!

SLOWLY RAISE IT UP OVER HIS HEAD.

HE WILL NATURALLY SIT DOWN.

SAY "GOOD DOG" AND GIVE HIM THE TREAT!

5-10-15

THAT'S ONE WAY TO GET YOUR DOG TO SIT.

ANOTHER WAY IS TO SAY "COME ON! IT'S TIME TO GO TO THE VET!"

FAGAN

21

Emily Dickinson

DRABBLE BY FAGAN

36

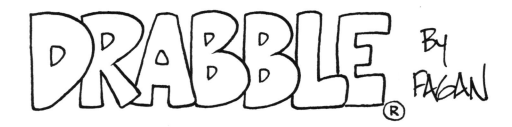

DRABBLE BY FAGAN

All Wally: A DRABBLE Book

55

KEVIN FAGAN

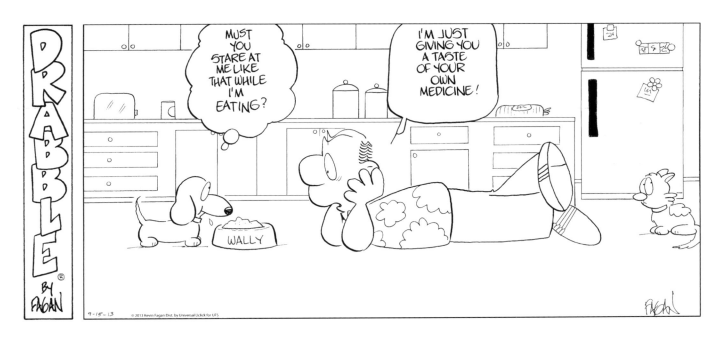

Wally's SUPERBOWL TERMINOLOGY

WALLY'S GUIDE TO WIENER DOGS 🐾

PLAYFUL

THAT'S ME!

CLEVER

I CAN GET YOU TO SHARE ANY TIME I WANT!

DEVOTED

I WAS ONLY GONE FOR TWO MINUTES!

3-24-15

FEARLESS

KNOCK KNOCK!

ROWF ROWF ROWF ROWF ROWF ROWF ROWF ROWF ROWF ROWF

I'M PRETTY SURE VETS DON'T MAKE HOUSE CALLS!

THE FAKE THROW IS THE ROTTENEST TRICK YOU CAN PLAY ON YOUR DOG!

3-25-15

WE TAKE OFF AFTER IT UNTIL WE REALIZE THE BALL IS STILL IN YOUR HAND!

IT'S SO EMBARRASSING! BUT JUST REMEMBER, I AM NOT STUPID!

!

I'LL ONLY FALL FOR THIS TRICK 15 OR 16 TIMES IN A ROW!

DON'T LET YOUR DOG PLAY WITH CAT TOYS!

DING DINGLE

3-26-15

FOR ONE THING, THEY ARE DISGUSTING BECAUSE THEY HAVE KITTY SPIT ALL OVER THEM!

FOR ANOTHER THING, DOGS LIKE TO CHEW THINGS UP, AND CAT TOYS CAN HAVE LITTLE BELLS AND OTHER STUPID THINGS INSIDE THEM!

AAKK

AND WATATEVER YOU DO, NEVER EVER GIVE A DOG TOY TO A CAT!

SWEET!

MINE!!

DRABBLE BY FAGAN

DRABBLE BY FAGAN

DRABBLE BY FAGAN

WHAT IN THE WORLD...

GO AWAY, WALLY! IT'S NOT TIME FOR YOUR BREAKFAST YET!

I KNOW YOU **THINK** IT'S TIME, BUT LAST NIGHT WE TURNED THE CLOCKS BACK ONE HOUR!

IN THE SPRING WE TURN IT UP AN HOUR, AND IN THE FALL WE TURN IT **BACK** AN HOUR!

11-2-14

I REALLY LOOK FORWARD TO THIS DAY BECAUSE I CAN SLEEP-IN!

© 2014 Kevin Fagan Dist. by Universal Uclick for UFS

I'LL WAIT HERE.

KEVIN FAGAN

98

KEVIN FAGAN

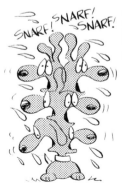

DRABBLE ® BY FAGAN

DRABBLE BY FAGAN

ABOUT THE AUTHOR

Kevin Fagan signed his first syndicate cartooning contract at age 21, and has been delighting newspaper audiences every day since then. That's over 14,000 original installments of DRABBLE!

DRABBLE characters include nerdy college student Norman, his father Ralph (the original mall cop), and mother Honeybunch. Norman's younger brother Patrick and little sister Penny round out the Drabble family. In addition to Wally the wiener dog, the other family pets are Oogie the cat and Bob the duck.

Follow Drabble in your local newspaper or at gocomics.com/drabble. Check out DrabbleComic on Facebook.com.

Made in the USA
San Bernardino, CA
22 November 2019

60266546R00071